FINDING HOPE AGAIN AFTER
THE DEATH OF A SPOUSE

Light
ON THE
HORIZON

LESLIE J. THOMPSON

What others are saying...

Suffering the loss of a spouse who is the love of your life is a profound and overwhelming grief. Leslie shares her own very raw experience of loss as she journaled her way through her despair. Her book, Light on the Horizon, offers comfort and hope to those facing similar challenges. Her writing is compassionate and insightful, and she has a genuine desire to help others find light in their own world. This book is a must read for anyone looking for a way through the darkness of grief.

ANDREA LENDE
Best-selling Christian author, speaker, and podcaster

For anyone experiencing the crushing loss of a loved one, Leslie J. Thompson's new book, Light on the Horizon, will bring light into those corners where the darkness of mourning thrives. Thompson is an experienced writer, one who leaves nothing unsaid. She writes of her husband's death with candor, touching on sweet memories in a collection of essays that are both personal and universal. This is a hope-filled book of recovery and forward motion. I strongly recommend it as a salve for the sorrow of loss, whether a spouse, a child, or a parent.

DEB DEARMOND
Multi-published award-winning author of books on family and marriage, including I Choose You Today - 31 Ways to Make Love Last and Don't Go to Bed Angry, Stay Up and Fight

Navigating grief is never easy and often takes longer than we want when we experience the loss of someone we love. Leslie J. Thompson weaves a story of hope when facing the hard and awful realities of death. Through her vulnerability, those who follow in her shoes will know they aren't alone, and the journey isn't impossible.

KAREN DEARMOND GARDNER
Speaker, advocate, and author of
Hope for Healing from Domestic Abuse

Leslie Thompson is a writer at heart, but with this book, she delivers more than a personal narrative. Instead, she gives us an intimate look deep into her heart, taking the reader from where she started in the difficult journey of grief to where she is now. Together, we experience her continued dependence on God and growth in His word. With transparency and honesty, she draws us into her reality. A must read for anyone who has experienced the loss of a loved one and for anyone desiring a deeper understanding of that heartbreak.

DONNA NABORS
Author of Shattered Dreams to Treasured Truths

Leslie's story opens a door into her heart of healing from the tragic loss of her husband. Trauma and grief are inevitable, yet Leslie refuses to shy away from their reality. She invites us to walk with her in a real-time process of pain, sorrow, God's love, anger, challenges, and most importantly, hope!

Leslie is brave, vulnerable, and faithful and gives each one of us permission to live in all of those spaces while navigating grief. No matter your story, Leslie's message will change you.

POLLY HAMP
Author, Trauma Recovery Coach,
and NLP Master Practitioner

Light ON THE
HORIZON

FINDING HOPE AGAIN AFTER
THE DEATH OF A SPOUSE

LESLIE J. THOMPSON

LIVING BRIDGE
PRESS

LIGHT ON THE HORIZON

Finding Hope Again After the Death of a Spouse

Copyright © 2023 by Leslie J. Thompson

ISBN: 979-8-9879704-0-9

Design by Kelly Surace.

To my fellow widows and all who grieve,
may you find peace in these pages
and hope in God's Word.

Contents

Foreword

I MET LESLIE THOMPSON THROUGH MUTUAL friends only a couple months after she lost her husband, Craig. In the four years since, I have personally witnessed her faith in action, as she walked day by day through the wilderness of grief toward a future full of promise.

In Leslie's latest work, she opens her heart and shares an intimate, genuine, and very personal journal that was a timeline of her tragedy. She honestly connects the reader to the human side of adversity while at the same time testifying to a very powerful glimpse into God's faithful presence along each step of the journey.

I was deeply moved by her many deep and profound insights into grief, which to me could have only come from the voice of God. Some were so profound, I found myself taking notes. I was also touched by how she faithfully honored her late husband along the way.

Leslie has been a living testimony of the faithfulness of God and a testimony of how one can, as the apostle Paul declared to the Philippians, "do all things through Christ who strengthens me." At the end of this book, I was left with an inspiring reminder of hope.

The love we experience in our temporary lives lasts for eternity. Though nothing will bring back Craig, we know, as with all our lost loved ones who professed faith in Christ Jesus, that a beautiful reunion lies on the other side. I am grateful for such a reminder and the powerful testament of a persistent and overcoming spirit Leslie has cultivated in her life.

ERIC SCHLEBUS
Senior Pastor
Grace Gathering Church
Sebastian, Florida

An Invitation

I LIVED MY GRIEF OUT LOUD. Month after month, I shared the raw reality of loss on my blog and social media, squinting to see the screen through a continual torrent of tears. Grief has a peculiar stigma because it makes people uncomfortable. It's grotesque. It can fester.

I needed to let it out.

As a writer, purging the heartache through words was the only thing that made sense. I was not seeking pity, but the public display of agony somehow brought me solace.

It also gave people hope. Although my musings were soaked in sorrow, they were rooted in faith. Something in me yearned to testify that my present loss did not negate God's eternal promise. In the wake of tragedy, I could still proclaim the good news of the gospel. Jesus came to give us life and life to the full. I would not let go of His garment.

I was preaching to myself in my posts, but others took note. Friends lauded my faith. Strangers found strength in my words. I discovered that encouraging others brought me joy. Even as my soul was in torment, I found purpose in the pain.

Jesus also became more real to me than ever before, a friend who sticks closer than a brother. My protector. My defender. My place of refuge and the lover of my soul. I wept, but I did not waver. Neither did He.

This book is a compilation of various writings documenting my journey of grief. They are a timeline that shows the progression from a heart shattered in pieces to one mended by God's love. They are a roadmap from the valley of despair to the mountain where He dwells.

I invite you to walk the journey with me, and I pray you are encouraged along the way. The letters on the page lead to the light on the horizon and a future full of promise. I also trust the One who walks with us will reveal Himself to you, and even as you press on along your own path, you will find rest for your soul. 💙

Let us hold fast the confession
of our hope without wavering,
for he who promised is faithful.
HEBREWS 10:23 (ESV)

Light ON THE HORIZON

The Backstory

MY HUSBAND AND BEST FRIEND—THE MAN who led me to the Lord and who chased fearlessly after Jesus—died on July 6, 2018. His death was the culmination of a decades-long battle with depression. Contrary to popular opinion, depression is not a matter of "wrong thinking," but rather an illness that attacks organs of the body—in this case the brain—in much the same way cancer does. And, like cancer, depression is a treatable disease that often can be managed or cured with changes in diet, nutritional supplements, counseling, and other methods. Craig fought depression with every fiber of his being, and he recorded a very powerful message about the battle in early June 2018, which he posted to his Facebook account. To date, the video has received more than 14,000 views.

Sadly, just like with cancer, depression can come out of remission and render the person helpless. Despite all their efforts and all the treatments, sometimes the disease wins. But that is no more a reflection of a person's character than if they were to succumb to any other illness. It is time we removed the stigma and talked candidly about depression and suicide.

The eulogy I delivered at Craig's memorial service came straight from the Holy Spirit. I received the message like a divine download about five days prior. The words flowed from my pen to the page with little effort and without the need to see clearly through pools of tears. I was blessed to honor God and honor my husband with these words less than two weeks after Craig's passing.

EULOGY FOR CRAIG BENNETT THOMPSON

In Psalm 139:13 – 14 (NASB 1995), the Psalmist King David writes:

FOR YOU FORMED MY INWARD PARTS;
YOU WOVE ME IN MY MOTHER'S WOMB.

I WILL GIVE THANKS TO YOU, FOR I AM
FEARFULLY AND WONDERFULLY MADE.

Craig Thompson was custom made for me in every way.

We met in 2003, when he was already thirty-eight years into his life's journey. It had not been an easy one. From the very beginning of our marriage, Craig was transparent with me about his struggles. He never hid his war wounds. But all I saw was an amazing man of God.

Craig was born in San Angelo, Texas and moved to Dallas as a child after his parents divorced. His father was an alcoholic, and his home environment was chaotic at best, traumatic at worst. Craig attended twelve different schools in eleven years and dropped out of high school in the eleventh grade after a guidance counselor told him he didn't have enough credits to graduate on time. Three decades later, that judgment still weighed heavy on him.

Which is incredibly ironic, because Craig is the most accomplished man I have ever met. After serving for six years in the United States Navy—which included three and a half years as a sumo wrestler to help build a cultural bridge between the U.S. and Japan—Craig worked as a private investigator and a hotel security manager, then ventured into the food and beverage industry before transitioning into software sales.

He left his last corporate job to pursue a lifelong dream of becoming a big band singer, because, you know, that's normal. And it was as "Big T" of Big T and the Bada-Bings that I first met him. Those of you who haven't heard the story of how God brought us together, catch me another time. It will rock your world, but it takes about ten minutes and we're on the clock.

Being married to Craig was the most thrilling adventure you could imagine. He was a consummate entrepreneur and we brought to life numerous business ventures he had conceived. We ran a retail store, started an insurance agency, launched two online television networks, then got into website design and mobile app development before diving headfirst into the drone world five years ago. Craig Thompson was a true Renaissance man.

But the most exhilarating part of all our many exploits was that Craig never met a stranger. He collected friendships every step of the way and years later still remembered the details of peoples' lives. He was also a natural-born encourager. For all his antics and sometimes off-color sense of humor, Craig loved to make people feel valued. He loved to help people overcome life's challenges and know that they were worth the fight.

And the more Craig matured in his faith, the more he was able to minister to others. The more he walked with God, the more he showed humility—he was able to touch people deep in their heart and soul because he was transparent about the pain of his own journey. People are hungry for authenticity, and Craig loved going deep.

Of course, being married to him, I was there behind the scenes during that process, and let me tell you, it was messy. We went through a very dark season in our marriage, with brutal verbal battles that created a whole fresh set of war wounds for both of us. It got really, really bad. But we didn't quit. In the darkest hour of our relationship, Craig made a beautiful video for our tenth anniversary and threw a surprise party for me with about eighty of our closest friends. We renewed our wedding vows, and from that point forward, Craig set the pace for healing in our hearts and our home.

He went on a five-day retreat called Quest to go deeper into his relationship with God, and he came back a changed man. I went on the women's version of the retreat three weeks later, because I wanted what he had. Peace and humility and the ability to listen without judgment. He was loving me so much better—doing the act of love through self-sacrifice—and that just made me want to love him better too.

He went on more retreats and started nurturing relationships with other amazing men of God who became brothers to him. Four years ago, Craig also discovered prison ministry and found a whole new set of brothers at the Powledge Unit that he would go to visit every single week.

Through all of this, I saw my husband—the man I already adored—become a mighty man of valor and, like the psalmist David, a man after God's own heart.

Craig loved people like no one else. He was raw and authentic—he was funny and goofy and also unafraid to tackle hard issues head-on. He loved me like no one else. I never could have dreamed of such an amazing husband. But, of course, God knew that. Ephesians 3:20 tells us that He gives us exceedingly, abundantly more than we can ask or think.

Craig had struggled with depression on and off for years, and I was blessed that we were coming off a really good run. The last four years of our marriage were amazing. I have the best husband. So, when the depression came back in the spring, I was committed to walking through the season together. It's like a cancer that comes back out of remission. It's not the person's fault they have cancer; it's something that happens to them.

But depression is more like an autoimmune disease. The body is an amazing machine, and it has systems in place to fight off intruders and keep itself healthy. But, if you have a disease like lupus or fibromyalgia or Type 1 diabetes, those systems turn on themselves. The body starts to attack itself. Depression does that to the brain. It is literally a malfunction—wrong thought patterns that can be exacerbated by a chemical and biological condition in which things are out of order, so that the mind turns on itself.

The disease of depression does not diminish Craig's legacy of love or his lust for life. Craig loved with passion and authenticity. He fought the depression with everything he had—he knew the battle he was facing, and he was absolutely determined to win. But just like with cancer, sometimes we lose.

Craig was the best husband, and he loved me so well. He loved me and loved others well because he loved God. If you don't know Jesus—know Him in the way that Craig knew Him and I know Him—I pray that you start today.

One of Craig's last journal entries was Philippians 1:6 (NLT), in which the apostle Paul writes:

> "AND I AM CERTAIN THAT GOD,
> WHO BEGAN THE GOOD WORK WITHIN YOU,
> WILL CONTINUE HIS WORK UNTIL IT IS FINALLY
> FINISHED ON THE DAY WHEN CHRIST JESUS RETURNS."

Jesus is coming back, and He is coming soon, before the great battle begins. I hope you will be with Him in the fight. But until He returns, God will continue to see through the great work that He began in Craig Thompson. He will see it through in me and in each one of you.

Jesus gave us two commandments:

> LOVE THE LORD YOUR GOD WITH ALL YOUR
> HEART AND WITH ALL YOUR SOUL AND WITH
> ALL YOUR STRENGTH AND WITH ALL YOUR MIND,
> AND, LOVE YOUR NEIGHBOR AS YOURSELF.
>
> LUKE 10:27 (NIV)

Craig loved me, and he loves you. Go love better.

The *light* shines in the darkness,
and the darkness has not overcome it.

JOHN 1:5 (ESV)

Ordinary Things

August 8, 2018 | **Day 33**

EVERY MORNING WHEN I WALK INTO the bathroom, Craig is there. His shaving cream and razor blades and hair gel are in the basket on the sink. His T-shirts and gym shorts are still folded neatly on top of the dresser in our closet. His sneakers stand at the ready by our bedroom door, so he can put them on for his morning walk to the park.

I cherish these things and have no plans to move them—much less remove them—anytime soon. A friend who lost her husband to suicide many years ago cleansed her house of all his belongings two days after laying him to rest. When she shared that recently, the very thought of it shook me to the core. Her experience was

9

different, of course, and everyone grieves in their own way. But I cannot fathom a home without Craig in every room. He is still very present, still very much a part of my every day. He is in the ordinary things.

Some may call this the denial stage. Grief has a recognizable pattern, after all, with denial being at the forefront. I prefer to call it anticipation. I am fully aware that Craig is not coming back. But I am equally aware that I will see him again soon. Will it be in our three-bedroom house in the Dallas suburbs? No. It will be when I go to join him and meet our Lord in the clouds. But until then, I have his things—the ordinary things—to remind me that we do have a future together, a glorious future more spectacular than I could ever imagine. And to remind me that he is still very much alive, more alive than ever before.

Praise be to the God and Father of our Lord Jesus Christ! In his great mercy he has given us new birth into a living hope through the resurrection of Jesus Christ from the dead, and into an inheritance that can never perish, spoil or fade (1 Peter 1:3-4).

We have a living hope in Jesus Christ. Scripture says we have this hope as an anchor for our soul, firm and secure. Although my heart is broken that my husband is in a room beyond the veil and I no longer can hear his voice, I rejoice in the knowledge that both he and I will spend eternity in the presence of the King of kings. As Craig wrote in his own epitaph:

> *Do not shed a tear or miss me for a moment, rather,*
> *Trust in the Lord Jesus the Christ as Your Savior,*
> *and you will join me soon in the Heavenly chorus*
> *of Worship of God Almighty.*

Craig is here. His love fills my heart. His presence fills our home. And God speaks to us through the ordinary things. 💙

Though you have not seen him, you love him; and even though you do not see him now, you believe in him and are filled with an inexpressible and glorious joy, for you are receiving the end result of your faith, the salvation of your souls.

1 PETER 1:8-9 (NIV)

A Kiss from My Husband

August 20, 2018

GOD SPEAKS TO ME IN NUMBERS. It started a couple of years ago with the 444s. I wouldn't have paid them much attention, except that my pastor's wife used to post them on Facebook once in a while. A picture of a license plate with 444, the time on the clock at 4:44PM. She called it a "God kiss." His way of letting her know that He was right there, that He sees her, and that He loves her.

At some point, I started getting 444s too. At first, I'd see one only occasionally; then I'd see number patterns more and more, like a flood. Undeniable. And I wasn't looking—they would always catch me by surprise. Later, I started to get 333. I heard more than once that this points to a specific passage of Scripture.

"Call to me and I will answer you and tell you great
and unsearchable things you do not know."

JEREMIAH 33:3 (NIV)

That's the New International Version (NIV). Other translations say, "great and indescribable things," "hidden things," or "incomprehensible things." The 3s in triplicate is God's way of calling us into deeper relationship. I started to get them all the time, and I was encouraged to press in.

In the last year, those conversations (God's and mine) around the numbers have expanded. He shows me times on the clock and calls me to look up Scriptures. Triplicates on license plates speak of His presence. I get 555 frequently, reminding me of His abiding grace. Grace upon grace upon grace. This spring, Craig started to get them, too. 333 and 444, all the time. Ironically, it miffed him at first—he claimed he didn't believe in the numbers. But they showed up with such regularity, he was beginning to doubt his own doubts. He would take screenshots of his phone and text me the picture. 3:33 PM. 4:44 AM. He, too, said he was never looking. He would just glance at the clock, and there would be God, waving hello.

I was delighted at this new turn of events and told him that the Father sees him and loves him! That God is revealing something magnificent to him, great and mighty things that he does not know. We were both listening attentively, with hope and anticipation. Especially, as the season grew dark.

I slept soundly last night but briefly awoke a couple hours after going to bed. I glanced at the clock. **1:13 AM**. I made a mental note and fell back asleep.

This morning, I eased into the day with Bible reading and scrolls through social media. Then the grief came, marked by a torrent of tears and heartache. I miss my husband. I feel lost. I journaled at length about how Craig taught me to love better. How we had both learned and grown so much these last several years. We discovered the joy in sacrifice—in trying to out-give one another by putting the other's needs and wants first. I still failed more times than I care to admit, but I was so much better. We were better. And we were happy.

I showered and got dressed. Sat on the floor of the closet holding one of Craig's T-shirts and sobbed. Took the dog for the walk and made breakfast. God reminded me to look up the time on the clock from last night, so I asked Google to find "Scripture 1:13." The answer brought more tears and likewise great comfort.

1 CORINTHIANS 13 (NIV)

If I speak in the tongues of men or of angels, but do not have love, I am only a resounding gong or a clanging cymbal. If I have the gift of prophecy and can fathom all mysteries and all knowledge, and if I have a faith that can move mountains, but do not have love, I am nothing. If I give all I possess to the poor and give over my body to hardship that I may boast, but do not have love, I gain nothing.

Love is patient, love is kind. It does not envy, it does not boast, it is not proud. It does not dishonor others, it is not self-seeking, it is not easily angered, it keeps no record of wrongs. Love does not delight in evil but rejoices with the truth. It always protects, always trusts, always hopes, always perseveres.

Love never fails. But where there are prophecies, they will cease; where there are tongues, they will be stilled; where there is knowledge, it will pass away. For we know in part and we prophesy in part, but when completeness comes, what is in part disappears. When I was a child, I talked like a child, I thought like a child, I reasoned like a child. When I became a man, I put the ways of childhood behind me. For now we see only a reflection as in a mirror; then we shall see face to face. Now I know in part; then I shall know fully, even as I am fully known.

And now these three remain: faith, hope and love. But the greatest of these is love.

God is faithful. And I have no doubt He is showing Craig great and mighty things. Hidden things that are unsearchable unless we are in His presence. What He is showing me is that I am still loved—loved more than I can ever fathom. And, in the same way that I discovered the delight in learning to love my husband, there is joy in loving others. In putting others' needs first. There is joy in loving God and putting His desires first.

Isaiah 54:5 (NIV) begins:

> *"For your Maker is your husband—*
> *the Lord Almighty is his name..."*

My husband gave me a kiss last night, and I am grateful. 💙

A Change of Season

January 13, 2019

WIDOWHOOD IS WEIRD. IT HAPPENS SUDDENLY, in an instant. One minute, you're married; the next minute, you're not. Your entire identity changes, and you have no control, no say in the matter.

A final breath. One last heartbeat. And then you are different. Everything is different. Widowhood is thrust upon you.

I tried to cook tonight. I boiled a bag of ready-made Thai rice and cut up some chicken tenders for a makeshift stir fry. I don't know anything about ingredients or flavor profiles. I squeezed a lemon over the chicken while it was in the pan and added salt and pepper. The other spices in the cupboard intimidate me. When all was said and done, I sat alone at the kitchen table and ate. The food was palatable, but far from flavorful. Afterward, I cried.

I cried because Craig was the chef in our home, and now he's gone. I cried because I not only loved his cooking, but I loved watching him cook. He enjoyed experimenting in the kitchen, like an artist playing with paint, and was an ardent Food Network fan. He could make the most incredible meals out of nothing.

When Craig visited me in New York City before we got married, he promptly sized up the meager provisions in my kitchen: four eggs, two Kaiser rolls, a cup of yogurt, a bottle of flat Coca-Cola, and a single-serving box of Cocoa Krispies. "Go hang out in there," he said, gesturing to the living area of my bite-size apartment. Only one person at a time could fit in the bantam kitchen, so I buried my nose in a book and listened to the clang of pots and the creak of the oven door from the other room. Some time later, Craig emerged with the most amazing bread pudding I have ever eaten.

To think, I was going to make fried eggs.

Now, very much alone in the house we shared, I gave myself a pep talk through the tears as I washed the cutting board and a single plate after my humble chicken entrée. "At least I tried," I said out loud. "I know he's proud, because at least I tried." But I didn't try, really. Trying would mean picking out a recipe and buying the right ingredients and preparing a meal with some forethought. My dinner was two steps up from ramen soup. Still, I used the stove and not the microwave, so that must count for something. And six months into this journey, I am continually learning to give myself grace.

Widowhood is weird, because it brings to light all the things you took for granted that in fact brought you the deepest joy and comfort. For weeks after Craig passed, I still listened for the creak of the banister when he came down the stairs in the morning. That was my cue to announce to the cats, "Daddy's awake!" and jump up from the couch to meet him in the kitchen. I would give him a good morning kiss and make his coffee while he wiped the sleep from his eyes. Then we would retreat to the living room and Craig would claim his usual spot on the love seat while I curled up on the sofa to read Scripture or surf social media.

I camped in that spot for a full week as visitors came to the house, bringing cookies and cakes and condolences. Friends sat with me and held my hand and insisted that I do nothing but just receive the love and kindness that was offered. On a few occasions, they gently asked for information about life insurance policies or sought my input on funeral arrangements. And they made sure I would eat.

I miss seeing my husband in the kitchen and on the couch and in the car and in our bed at night. I miss our conversations and his mannerisms and knowing he was always a text or a call or mere steps away. I miss the rhythms of daily life, even with our unpredictable schedule, and the certainty that we would face together whatever challenges were in store. And I miss being a wife. His wife. The story of how we met and married was our joint testimony of God's awesome power and perfect plan. We would tell it in tandem—me sharing my part, and Craig chiming in with his—and the reaction was always the same. People knew God was real and that we were meant for each other.

Widowhood hasn't quite sunk in yet; I'm not sure it ever will. I still consider myself Craig's wife and often speak of him in the present tense. Even so, he would be the first to tell me that my true identity is not as his bride, but as a daughter of the Most High King. Years ago, Craig wrote me a letter in which he poured out his heart and shared his deep and unwavering love for me. "The only one who loves you more is our Father in heaven," he said.

The seasons may change, but my identity has not. I am still a bride. I am still a daughter. And I am still deeply loved beyond all measure. My husband is in the Father's house. I will see him again soon enough, and together we will stand before our Lord and King. Until then, I will crack open a cookbook, and I will try something new. 💙

Give Thanks Always

February 14, 2019

THIS VALENTINE'S DAY IS FULL OF IRONIES. The irony that Craig and I never really did much for Valentine's Day the past few years, yet his absence is profound. The irony that I loved him with all my heart while he was alive and discovered an even deeper love after he was gone. The irony that Craig and I shared a passion for travel, and he adored tropical landscapes, and here I am in Nicaragua marking the most romantic holiday with two fellow widows.

Our stories are eerily similar. We each had husbands who demonstrated a heart for God, a zest for life, an unwavering love toward us, and extravagant compassion and generosity toward others. And we each lost our husband to suicide.

I woke up today at 4:00 AM for no particular reason, other than the restlessness in my soul. I felt the emotional churn of overflowing joy mixed with deep sadness. I am on a fun-filled vacation in a beautiful country with two amazing women...but my husband is not by my side. Even so, I thank God upon every remembrance of him, and I am blessed beyond words at how our sweet Father continues to minister to me. He has brought me new friends. He has taken me on new adventures. He has given me new life. The Lord is my shepherd; I lack nothing.

So today, I give thanks. Thank You, Father, for the gift of fourteen years of marriage to the most amazing man on earth, custom built just for me. Thank You for teaching me about love and compassion and empathy through his example and our shared journey of healing. Thank You for never leaving me alone, not for one single minute, during this time of transition. Thank You, God, for making streams in the wilderness. 💙

The LORD is my shepherd; I shall not want.
He makes me lie down in green pastures.
He leads me beside still waters.
He restores my soul.
PSALM 23:1-3A (ESV)

The Wonder of The Journey

February 16, 2019

CRAIG AND I TRAVELED EXTENSIVELY DURING our marriage—for work, for pleasure, and on a couple of mission trips. He taught me to "wear each day like a loose garment." Make plans, sure, but don't get bent out of shape when things don't go your way—when flights are delayed, or events are cancelled, or people are rude. "We'll get there," he would say. "Enjoy the journey."

The drive from San Juan del Sur to the artisan's market at Masaya this morning took a little more than two hours. In terms of distance, the drive time could have been half that, but the trip is an exercise in patience. You're constantly dodging bicyclists and mopeds traveling along the side of the road and waiting for brief windows of opportunity to dart around slow-moving trucks, tractors, and horse-drawn carts. We drove past fields of sugar cane and plantain trees, past teensy cinderblock and stucco homes with sheet tin roofs, lush foliage, parched farms, skinny oxen, and herds of goats grazing in the shade. Roadside fruit stands beckoned outside the town of Rivas, and several enterprising food vendors descended upon our SUV when we stopped for gas. The people, the vehicles, the landscape all gave no room for hurry. Schedules are a loosely held concept, not a mandate.

I remembered Craig's wise counsel as I felt God whisper to my soul. "Relax. You will reach your destination soon enough. Set aside your plans and expectations. Discover the wonder of the journey." I expect new discoveries await in this journey of widowhood too. 💙

Throughout all their journeys,
whenever the cloud was taken up from over the tabernacle,
the people of Israel would set out.

EXODUS 40:36 (ESV)

Why are you cast down, O my soul,
and why are you in turmoil within me?
Hope in God;
for I shall again praise him,
my salvation and my God.

PSALM 42:5 (ESV)

Tostones for One

February 17, 2019

SHORTLY AFTER CRAIG'S PASSING, A GOOD friend told me that grief and joy are not mutually exclusive. You can be both happy and sad. You can savor the present moment while mourning what was lost. You can just...be.

The past six days in Nicaragua have been magical, fun, healing, and full of adventure. I have enjoyed every minute discovering new landscapes with new friends. And I have cried. I cried while soaking in the pool looking out over a quiet lagoon nestled in the crater of a dormant volcano. I cried while slipping under crisp sheets in a queen-size bed at a luxury eco lodge. I cried ordering tostones con queso at the airport, waiting to board my flight back to the States. I have cried because it's just me. Because texting photos to your mom and your best friends isn't the same as texting them to your husband. Because a hundred Facebook likes won't bring him back.

I am happy and sad, full of joy and full of grief. I am his, and I am His. And I know that both Craig and God are cheering me on as I lean forward. Smiling. Crying. Pressing on. 💙

Yet what we suffer now is nothing
compared to the glory he will reveal to us later.
ROMANS 8:18 (NLT)

Hidden Treasures

February 23, 2019

A WEEK AGO, I MOVED CRAIG'S toiletries case into the bathroom closet. The act took little physical energy, yet it felt like a Herculean feat. Something so trivial carried such significance— putting away the past, shutting up expectations. I hated making the decision, but it was one more small step toward healing.

People walk out their grief in different ways. A friend from church visits her son's grave weekly. I have been to Craig's only once in seven months. Another friend got rid of all her husband's clothing the weekend they buried him. My father has been gone eleven years, and my stepmother still has many of his belongings.

Last night, I opened the dresser drawer that holds Craig's undershirts and sobbed. Day after day, week after week, those shirts went into the laundry and came out renewed. I prided myself on my folding technique as I pulled them from the dryer. I always packed at least one extra in Craig's suitcase when he traveled, in case of contingency. They looked up at me from inside the dresser drawer with blank stares. At least a dozen white V-necks, neatly folded. Dormant.

Pulling Craig's travel case back out of the closet this morning felt almost sacrilegious. The small canvas case might as well have housed the crown jewels. I handled it with great reverence and a heavy heart, plucking the tweezers from a zippered pouch inside before returning the bag to its new home.

I am a slow walker when it comes to grief. Or maybe not. Others might say I am speeding along at a breakneck pace—that I am so much more healed and whole than they were seven months out. The pace doesn't much matter, I suppose, as long as one keeps moving forward. Forging ahead. Taking one more small step toward healing. 💙

But lay up for yourselves treasures in heaven,
where neither moth nor rust destroys
and where thieves do not break in and steal.

MATTHEW 6:20 (ESV)

Sucker Punched

February 23, 2019

IN THE FIRST DAYS AND WEEKS after Craig passed, well-meaning friends struggled to find words of solace. Many understood that experiencing the fullness of sorrow can be healing, while others longed to offer comfort and hope by looking ahead toward a future beyond the searing pain. A phrase I heard more than once (and loathed from the start) was that, in time, I would adapt to "the new normal."

For someone in the throes of grief, those words are a kick in the gut. The very idea of life without the person you have lost is an insult to the senses. Suggesting that their absence could in any way eventually feel "normal" struck me as both disrespectful and dishonest.

The word "normal" also carries with it some measure of certainty. Normal is predictable; it is commonplace. But grief, by its very nature, is disruptive. Grief creates chaos and turns life upside down, and though it may lessen over time, it never really leaves. It lurks in landscapes and photos and familiar smells. Months or years after the initial loss, grief shows up and throws a sucker punch.

I had plenty on my mind yesterday while I was driving to a local production studio for a video shoot. I had made sure to copy the client's script onto a USB drive and bring a portable hard drive with me to transfer the footage. Speeding along the President George Bush Turnpike, I calculated how much time I would need to edit the video later that afternoon and contemplated grabbing takeout on my way home. All was right with the world as I exited onto Trinity Mills Road. And then it wasn't.

I suddenly realized I was driving toward Addison Airport—the same route Craig and I used to take at least once a week when he got his pilot's license back in 2015. Every building and tree was seared into my memory. I could picture the chairs and the coffee machine and the small fridge with bottled water in the hanger where I would wait for Craig—feeling equal parts anxious and proud—while he would go up with his flight instructor. On the drive home, I would ask him to tell me everything he had learned and listen attentively as he rolled through the details.

Getting his pilot's license had been a lifelong dream, but Craig only pursued it after we started our aerial video business to meet FAA requirements for commercial drone operators. He was harder on himself than necessary as he completed his flight training and, ultimately, passed the exam with ease. I flew with him only twice. What I wouldn't give for just one more hour in the air together.

As I turned onto Midway Road, I could see a small plane overhead coming in for a landing on the airstrip a few hundred yards away. Memories came flooding back and tears trickled down my cheeks. "Ow, Daddy. Ow, ow, ow," I said out loud, telling God plainly how much the grief hurt my heart. I took several deep breaths, knowing I needed to pull myself together by the time I made it to the studio. "It still hurts so bad," I muttered. Where was this font of pain coming from? I felt ambushed.

But, by the time I walked into the studio, I was all smiles. The camera operator had never met Craig, and I saw no reason to burden him with my grief. We had work to do. Part of my job also is to put the client and crew at ease to ensure everything goes smoothly. Feelings would have to wait.

At times, I lean into the heartache, wringing tears from my eyes in honor of my husband. For the most part, however, I choose not to wallow in sadness. I have people to see and places to go. Grief took a cheap shot yesterday. It coldcocked me in the car. But I'm still standing. Those many memories, albeit painful, keep Craig front-of-mind. For that, I am grateful. Our adventures made me who I am today. Although I will never accept his absence as "normal," I have learned to navigate the sadness—to tuck away my tears, when needed, and to freely let them flow at home or with friends. I have learned that grief strips away all pretense to bring us closer to others. And I have learned that, despite my reticence, there indeed is a future beyond the searing pain. 💙

"For I know the plans I have for you," declares the LORD,
"plans to prosper you and not to harm you,
plans to give you hope and a future."
JEREMIAH 29:11 (NIV)

Figure Eight

March 6, 2019

8 MONTHS.

Eight. Months.

Without my best friend.

Without my business partner.

Without a kiss goodnight.

Without a morning hug.

Eight months of moving forward, going places, getting things done. And still waiting.

Waiting for the dream that feels like time travel. Waiting for the day I come home and there you are, because none of it was real.

Waiting for the trumpet sound.

I cry in the car and on the couch and in the shower. I cry in the quiet hours and the safe spaces. And then I move forward. I make plans and go places and I laugh and smile. Because God is good.

I have new friends and deeper relationships. I have seen new places and more adventures lie ahead. I have a new sense of purpose and a fresh calling. I am deeply loved by my Father, by Craig, and by an army of amazing people. I cannot help but to be grateful. So today, I will mark eight months by doing what my husband did so well.

Today, I will go love more. 💙

Therefore, since we are surrounded by such a great cloud of witnesses, let us throw off everything that hinders and the sin that so easily entangles. And let us run with perseverance the race marked out for us.

HEBREWS 12:1 (NIV)

An Almost Perfect Walk

April 20, 2019

I WAS PREPARED FOR BATTLE THIS morning. Sunglasses. Handkerchief. Cell phone fully charged. I expected pain. I expected warfare. I expected to revisit a place of suffering and toil by retracing my husband's steps during his battle against depression.

Instead, I took a walk.

I knew I was going for a walk, of course. But this was a meaningful walk, and the decision to go had been weighty. This morning was my first time walking to the park a half mile from our house—the park that Craig and I walked to together at least a dozen times in the weeks before he died last summer. The park where he sat on a bench in the shade and recorded a four-minute video in which he poured out his heart, begging viewers to stand strong against the lies of the enemy. A spirit of suicide was sweeping the nation, taking out notable figures like Kate Spade and Anthony Bourdain, along with thousands of teenagers and adults who had succumbed to depression. Craig was wrestling with it as well, and our daily power walk was a weapon in his arsenal. Exercise releases endorphins, reducing the perception of pain. We had a plan. We could beat this.

Four weeks later, Craig lost the fight. And I stopped going to the park.

I always loved to walk. I spent part of my youth in Germany and a decade in Manhattan; walking for me was a way of life. It felt as natural as breathing, and almost as necessary. The first year of our marriage, Craig and I took early morning walks around the golf course near our apartment complex, sharing thoughts and dreams as we became more closely knit as a couple. Walking was good exercise, but for me, it was about connection. Those walks fueled my love for my husband and refreshed my soul.

After we moved to our house, we rarely walked together. Occasionally, Craig would join me to take the dog around the block, or humor me by strolling through a street fair. I could trick him into walking when we went to Six Flags amusement park or traveled on vacation. But for the most part, walking was my thing, not his. So, I was pleasantly surprised last spring when he asked me for a suggested route to walk for forty-five minutes. Two laps through the back alleys around our neighborhood and one time around the inner loop would do the trick, I replied, then realized just how mundane that path would be. Craig looked dismayed. "Or, you could walk to the park and do a loop around the trails. That's probably forty-five minutes there and back," I said.

He set out the next morning on his own, returning home drenched in sweat. The following day, he was off again, strengthening muscles, building a routine. I was envious. After the first week, I asked whether I could join him. Sure, he said. What for him felt strenuous was for me pure bliss. Walking with my husband—my favorite person of all time. He stayed laser focused on keeping a brisk pace. I focused on speaking life over him, reminding him of his calling and God's promises. We were in the fight together, us against the world.

Do not be anxious about anything, but in every situation,
by prayer and petition, with thanksgiving,
make your requests known to God.
And the peace of God, which transcends all understanding,
will guard your hearts and minds in Christ Jesus.

PHILIPPIANS 4:6-7 (NIV)

I thought about the park several times after Craig passed. How much I loved being out in nature, breathing the fresh air. I thought about keeping up the routine but always found an excuse. The late summer was too hot, I was traveling in the fall, and winter was cold and dreary.

But now, it's spring. Birds are chirping. Everything is green. I had nothing on my calendar. Today was the perfect day for a walk in the park.

I wore my sunglasses as I left the house, and the tears came quickly. They trickled down my cheeks as I turned left onto the main road. The first two blocks slope downhill, and gravity propelled me along. Dogs barked behind fences. A crow swooped low overhead. I sang softly to myself as I walked, settling my mind, picking up details. The world was in Technicolor.

As I neared the park, I could see people gathered around a canopy tent by the tree line. Hundreds of plastic eggs were strewn across the grass nearby. Tomorrow is Easter Sunday, and families were there to celebrate. The children paced in anticipation, baskets at the ready, eyeing their bounty. They were waiting for permission to run. So was I.

I kept bracing for the pain, anticipating grief. But it never came. Instead, I was captivated by the beautiful scenery and the bright sunshine and the cool breeze. The trails were empty, the atmosphere serene. I couldn't help myself—I was happy. Halfway around the loop, I decided to embrace the joy. What a spectacular morning. Perfect weather, and the perfect day for a walk. I wished Craig were with me, but I knew my Husband was there. Jesus was right by my side. How else could I explain the peace in my soul?

You will forget the shame of your youth
and remember no more the reproach of your widowhood.
For your Maker is your husband—the LORD Almighty is his name

ISAIAH 54:4B–5A (NIV)

Whether I will make a walk to the park part of my daily routine remains to be seen. What I know for certain, however, is that I never walk alone. I am grateful for God's unfailing love and for the comforting arms of my Savior. Jesus spent three days in the tomb—Scripture tells us He was a man of sorrows and acquainted with grief. He is not afraid to walk with us through seasons of darkness. And He walks us back out. The same Spirit that raised Jesus from the dead lives in me. Today, I took a walk. Tomorrow is resurrection day. 💙

For everything there is a season,
and a time for every matter under heaven.
ECCLESIASTES 3:1 (ESV)

Though you have made me see troubles,
many and bitter,
you will restore my life again;
from the depths of the earth
you will again bring me up.
You will increase my honor
and comfort me once more.

PSALM 71:20-21 (NIV)

A Story Stroll

May 6, 2019

TODAY IS TEN MONTHS SINCE CRAIG DIED. I have pondered this milestone for the past week—what it might feel like, and whether I should do anything special to celebrate him. I considered recording a video, and I might still, but I had neither the time nor the mental bandwidth this morning to gather my thoughts. So, I opted for a walk.

A walk would provide a time of quiet reflection—the perfect way to honor the occasion. I could walk to the park and follow the winding trail through the woods where Craig and I journeyed together last spring. I would enjoy the sights and sounds of nature and think about those last precious days with my husband as I retraced our steps.

Of course, God had other plans.

I arrived at the park to discover the sidewalk was closed. The earth had been torn up and a team of workers was installing large pipes underground. Signs pointed to an alternate route, and I veered toward the new course, realizing I didn't have much choice. How appropriate that I would encounter an unexpected detour on the day I was commemorating Craig's death—the most unexpected detour of all.

The new path took me past the playground, which was surprisingly empty, and around a cluster of trees before connecting back to the familiar trail. I noticed the city had installed new signs every few feet along the path, inviting children and visitors to take a "Story Stroll." Each station invited kids to notice interesting things in their surroundings, explore new places, and imagine the possibilities.

God whispered: ***This is a new story.***

I walked through the woods, doing only the inner loop and not the full power walk that Craig and I took together. That path was meant to work up a sweat and shake loose the darkness that had taken hold of his mind. This walk was meant for reminiscing. I did not need to hurry. Nothing needed fixing.

In the center of the trees, I caught the delicious scent of honeysuckle. My eyes scanned the branches and brambles for the source, and I spotted the wild vines a few feet farther down the trail. The memories came swiftly and made me smile. Honeysuckle grew along the driveway of the house where I grew up, and I smelled it every day when I came home from school. I was a latchkey kid and learned at an early age to fend for myself. The sweet aroma was a gentle reminder: I know how to be alone.

Jesus said, "Let the little children come to me, and do not hinder them,
for the kingdom of heaven belongs to such as these."

MATTHEW 19:14 (NIV)

Making my way back toward the main road, I was happy to see a mother and her children had staked claim to the playground. I decided to leave the park through the main exit, rather than walk back to the path that Craig and I used to follow. God spoke to my heart again. You don't have to retrace your steps. Both routes would lead me home.

Ten months in, I am learning to accept the unplanned, to walk boldly along the alternate route. God wants to take me someplace new, and there is beauty in the detour. 💙

Trust in the Lord with all your heart,
And lean not on your own understanding;
In all your ways acknowledge Him,
And He shall direct your paths.
PROVERBS 3:5-6 (NKJV)

Unstuck

June 13, 2019

IN MY EARLY TEENS, I WENT on a memorable trip to Cuxhaven, a small town on the north coast of Germany. Ironically, I don't recall whether I traveled with classmates or my family, but the trip itself has stuck in my mind—stuck being the operative word.

Droves of tourists travel to Cuxhaven each year to visit the Wadden Sea National Park and enjoy the cathartic experience of wading through mud. When the tide rolls out along the coast, the seabed turns from sandy loam to viscous slime. The mud extends hundreds of yards out to the horizon, making it possible to slog one's way on foot across the tidal flats to small dune islands offshore. Mudflat hiking is both exhilarating and exhausting and feels not unlike walking through quicksand (although not as perilous). With each step, you sink into the wet earth, the muck rising above your ankles. Lunging forward, you wait for the ground to stabilize beneath your toes, then extricate your other foot and continue plodding along.

The brisk sea air and swooping gulls provide pleasant distractions along the journey, but once in a while, the mudflat catches you in its grip. In those moments, you humbly extend a hand and ask a fellow traveler for added leverage to help you get unstuck. You shouldn't walk alone.

For the past year, I have waded through the mire—trudging forward, day by day, in the wake of losing my husband. At times, each step required my full focus as I wriggled free from the sticky grief to forge ahead. Other days, I chose to rest and listen to the sound of birds and distant waves while savoring the cool breeze on my face. Standing firm in unfamiliar surroundings, I experienced brief but not infrequent moments of beauty and peace. And daily, without fail, God was there to pull me out of the mud. To keep me from being trapped in my circumstance.

He did it through the prayers uttered by friends and strangers, through hugs in church pews and laughter in coffee shops. When I extended my hands to the heavens in the quiet morning hours or gripped my pillow in the dead of night, He was there. A gentle pull, a whisper of strength. Another step.

The ebb and flow of the North Sea tide is constant. Eventually, the waters move in again, nudging wanderers back toward the shore. Mud gives way to solid ground, and you can pick up the pace. Aching muscles and wobbly steps still bear witness to the challenge of the journey, but in time, you resume your stride. Each step comes without thinking, and you can walk freely again. Lighter. Stronger. Unstuck. 💙

I waited patiently for the Lord;
he inclined to me and heard my cry.
He drew me up from the pit of destruction,
out of the miry bog,
and set my feet upon a rock,
making my steps secure.

PSALM 40:1-2 (ESV)

As The Day Approaches

July 1, 2019

I CAN SEE THE MILESTONE ON the near horizon. One year. A whole year. Where I used to count up—one week, one month, six months—now I've been counting down. Saturday will be 365 days since Craig passed. One year since my world changed. A year of transition, revelation, deep sorrow, and occasional joy.

One year.

Others have been counting too. Friends and acquaintances have reached out this past week with words of comfort and concern. "How are you doing with the big day coming up?" "Do you have anything planned that day?" Their questions are rooted in sincerity and deep compassion. Yet, I found myself texting a fellow widow to ask, "Is it normal to want to punch them in the throat?"

I am an ingrate. But grief is not logical. My friend affirmed my mudpuddle of emotions and shared from her own journey. The end of her text summarized so perfectly my feelings as I watch the days and hours tick by.

"There's no such thing as an easy answer to these types of questions. If I say I'm doing well, then I'm lying. But there's no way for me to succinctly explain to you something you just can't understand if you haven't experienced it," she wrote.

Yes. That.

Truthfully, though, I am doing well. Last week was marked by two days of crippling grief and brain fog. But yesterday was brilliant. I watched a friend's son get baptized. A midday video shoot for a long-time client went exceptionally well. In the evening, nearly twenty people gathered at my home for food and fellowship, healing prayer, and a time of teaching in God's Word. The day was a series of successes and cause for celebration. I cried briefly as I said goodnight to my absent husband, but I went to bed grateful. I dare say, I felt content.

> *And let us consider how we may spur one another on toward love and good deeds, not giving up meeting together, as some are in the habit of doing, but encouraging one another— and all the more as you see the Day approaching.*
>
> HEBREWS 10:24-25 (NIV)

Life is a series of mile markers. Some bring great joy—graduations and weddings, new homes, new jobs, new births. Others mark times of sadness and loss. The death of a parent. The death of a spouse. The death of a dream. But the journey does not stop at the milestones. They are simply indicators of the profound events along the way and point to the road ahead. They shape our perspective as we look back and look forward, while helping us to find our place in the present.

And so, I face the road boldly and encourage myself with the promises in God's Word. He gives us beauty for ashes, the oil of joy for mourning, the garment of praise for the spirit of despair. Yes, this is my temporary home. But who knows what milestones lie beyond the next hill and what the next sunrise will bring?

The Spirit of the Sovereign Lord is on me,
because the Lord has anointed me
to proclaim good news to the poor.
He has sent me to bind up the brokenhearted,
to proclaim freedom for the captives
and release from darkness for the prisoners,
to proclaim the year of the Lord's favor
and the day of vengeance of our God,
to comfort all who mourn,
and provide for those who grieve in Zion—
to bestow on them a crown of beauty
instead of ashes,
the oil of joy
instead of mourning,
and a garment of praise
instead of a spirit of despair.
They will be called oaks of righteousness,
a planting of the Lord
for the display of his splendor.

ISAIAH 61:1-3 (NIV)

Fourteen Months

September 6, 2019

I LET THE DOG OUT THIS morning and looked up at the waning stars. The day was still quiet, but dawn was fast approaching. Another milestone.

"I never would have imagined," I said out loud to no one. A brief sense of defeat washed over me as I watched our Jack Russell go about her routine. She turned toward the door, ready for a treat. And I counted my blessings.

Today marks fourteen months since Craig crossed over to a world we cannot see. Rather than mourn, I reflected on what God has done. In fourteen months, I have been to Nicaragua and Guatemala, to Florida and Oregon and Kentucky. I have celebrated family gatherings in the summer and the fall, eaten pizza on the beach, and discovered the beauty of Lake Michigan. I have helped a longtime friend get back on her feet while I learned to walk again myself, hosted small group meetings in my home, and sponsored a table in Craig's honor at a benefit dinner. I have stayed engaged in women's Bible study, prison ministry, and the Rotary Club, and soaked up buckets of love and support from friends old and new in each of those realms. I have reconnected with former classmates and coworkers, prayed over the sick, painted the bedroom, and celebrated Passover.

I have cried more in fourteen months than in the fourteen years prior. But those tears watered the roots of my faith. Losing my earthly husband spurred a deeper intimacy with my Creator and a hunger for His Word. And as I have pressed into Him, I have experienced His boundless love in surprising new ways. He whispers to my heart, shows me special signs, and sweetly demonstrates His care through all those who continue to rally around me when I fear I've been forgotten.

Yesterday, I received a letter from an inmate whom I met through prison ministry. His name is Hezekiah, and he is eighty-five years old. I admired the beautiful cursive penmanship as I read his words of encouragement. "Since your husband Craig has been summoned by the Lord to another area of glory, the Lord has challenged me to check on you," he wrote. He reminded me that some days may feel more burdensome than others, but God will never leave me or forsake me. The joy of the Lord is my strength.

Hebrews 13:3 says, "Remember those in prison, as if you were their fellow prisoner." How could my heart not leap at his note? This precious man, who has spent decades behind bars, knew the danger of being bound by grief and self-pity, and he remembered me. He remembered me.

I still count the days, but I also count my blessings. I have walked fourteen months without my husband, but I had fourteen years of marriage with him. I am so grateful for the adventures and laughter and lessons we learned. If it weren't for Craig, I never would have met Hezekiah or all the other brothers in Christ behind bars, or all my friends at Rotary, or everyone I know through retreats we attended and ministries we support, or even our neighbors next door. Craig had an unwavering passion for people and lived to love others. Today, I will honor him by doing the same. 💙

A time to weep, and a time to laugh;
a time to mourn, and a time to dance...
ECCLESIASTES 3:4 (ESV)

Breath of Life

September 26, 2019

EARLIER THIS WEEK, I DISCOVERED AN unusual video that my husband left behind. He was testing a new camera gimbal and recorded jerky footage of our living room furniture as he fiddled with various settings on the remote control. I watched eagerly, waiting for a greater narrative to unfold, but Craig had switched off the camera after less than a minute. Others may have found the footage unremarkable. To me, it was priceless.

I could hear him breathing.

The sound of Craig's breath gripped my heart as if he were reading me a love poem. Every inhalation, every sigh, had been imprinted in my soul during our fourteen years of marriage.

I recognized the slight huff as he lifted the camera and the way his breathing changed when he was problem-solving. I listened to the air flow from his lungs as he went about his work and pictured the way he pursed his lips while deep in thought. The tears came.

We take so much for granted with the people we hold dear. Their mannerisms. Their gait. The sound and cadence of their voice. We tacitly cherish those qualities yet rarely give them any thought. For fourteen years, I laid next to my husband in bed at night, quietly comforted by the sound of his breathing. Those times he would snore, I preferred to forego sleep rather than have him move to the couch. Even when we fought, I wanted him near. Next to me. Sighing deeply.

In the creation story, God formed man from the dust of the ground and breathed into his nostrils the very breath of life. Whereas God had spoken the rest of creation into existence, man was different. God's divine breath made Adam a living being.

I could hear the breath of life in that video—the wind from Craig's mouth carrying the melody of his spirit. That haphazard scene of the living room couch reveals how his presence once filled our home, even when no words were spoken. I will listen to it again someday and cherish a sound I hadn't much considered before. It's a sound we should never take lightly, as each breath holds the essence of someone we love. 💙

The Spirit of God has made me,
and the breath of the Almighty gives me life.

JOB 33:4 (ESV)

Lasting Impressions

October 21, 2019

I STOOD IN HIS SHOES TONIGHT.

I was hanging up clothes after getting changed for bed and looked at Craig's side of the closet. Everything is still as it was the day he died, save for a few things I'd given a former inmate we knew from prison ministry. I scooped my arms around a cluster of shirts and rested my head against the fabric. The hangers underneath felt nothing like Craig's shoulder, and his scent was long gone, but I clung tightly to the memories.

Looking down, I noticed his flip-flops on the carpet. They were a staple of his summer wardrobe, along with his dark grey sneakers and the leather sandals he had on when he passed. The sneakers are still in the same spot by the bedroom door where he left them the morning of July 6, 2018, after working out. I nudge them here and there during the week, and I relocated them for a day when I had the flooring replaced. But for now, they still live by the door, offering the illusion of normalcy.

I hadn't given Craig's flip-flops much thought before this evening, but standing in the closet, I saw them in a new light. How could I have overlooked their value? Because the last things to touch the padding of those flip-flops were the soles of his feet.

I slipped my right foot into the oversized shoe, navigating my toes into place, then stepped into its mate. My skin touched where his once was. It was the closest I could get to touching him again. I closed my eyes and let quiet tears fall as my feet nestled into the impressions he'd left behind.

He stood here.

Probably not here in the closet, of course. Odds are, I'd picked up his shoes from downstairs and put them away while Craig was busy at the computer or watching TV. But he had stood in these sandals with his bare feet, and they had been shaped by his weight and his walk. So, I stood in them, too, hoping to absorb any remnant of his DNA through my skin as I felt the weight of my grief.

Moments later, I stepped back onto the carpet and wiped away the tears. Self-pity is always lurking in the wings, along with the temptation to hide in dark places. But those flip-flops had not lived in the closet. They'd been on walks through the neighborhood and trips to the pool and vacations in Mexico. They were meant for the sun.

Craig loved people. He used food and travel and new technologies as entry points for deeper conversations and lasting connections. An extrovert and an encourager, he touched countless lives. Standing in his shoes, I reflected on the journey that we walked together, and how he always challenged me to step out of my comfort zone.

Even now, I hear him cheering me on from the rafters, telling me to keep moving. Where grief wants to stay stuck, he says there is more to come. I am walking through unfamiliar terrain these days, but I am never alone. The Lord continues to guide my steps, and I trust in Him. So in the morning, I will get up and get dressed, slipping on my own shoes to pursue God's promises. Because each day brings a fresh opportunity to connect with others in hopes that I, too, can leave a lasting impression. 💙

For you have delivered me from death and my feet from stumbling,
that I may walk before God in the light of life.

PSALM 56:13 (NIV)

Even though I walk through the valley of the shadow of death,
I will fear no evil, for you are with me;
your rod and your staff, they comfort me.

PSALM 23:4 (ESV)

Washed Clean

I CRIED GOING THROUGH THE CAR wash today. I cried because for the third time in a year, I had just come from Discount Tire, where they fixed a flat caused by a rogue nail, and although I continue to prove that I am perfectly capable of managing life without Craig, I don't like it one bit.

Later in the evening, I cried standing in the kitchen while eating clementines, because although I'm perfectly capable of cooking, I don't enjoy it, and the one who really did isn't here to prepare a delicious dinner that would be a direct expression of both his culinary creativity and his love.

Yesterday, I cried when I met with my counselor, because I had muscled through the holidays and Craig's birthday and I was still standing but he was still gone and that wasn't going to change and my heart is in pieces.

Yet, amid all the tears, I am reminded daily of God's love and His faithfulness. I am reminded that He's not done with me yet, and if nothing else, the fact that I keep going can give someone else hope and that's all the reason I need. Every day, the deep ache in my heart reminds me of God's greatest blessing in my life—the man who led me to Christ and then became my husband and helped me become a better version of myself.

For years, Craig was the one who took the cars to get washed. I knew that I should at least take mine sometimes, but I was scared. I didn't trust myself to drive into the track that locks in your wheel and automatically guides your car through the wash, and so I never went. Instead, I let Craig demonstrate his thoughtfulness month after month, knowing in the back of my mind that I wasn't pulling my weight. When he started traveling for work and the days that he was home became a special treat, my desire to show my appreciation outweighed my anxiety. I went to the car wash by myself.

It seems like such a small thing, but for me it was huge—I was facing my fears, because he was worth fighting for. And Craig also knew that what seemed like a menial task was, in fact, an expression of sacrificial love. Little things mean a lot.

So, I cried today as I rode through the car wash, watching through watery eyes as suds covered the windshield. I hoped Craig was proud, because I was doing menial things and harder things and not letting circumstances throw me off course. And I cried in the kitchen not because I was eating clementines for dinner or couldn't cook a meal, but because the house is so quiet and life is just really, really boring without him.

I can't change this present reality, and acceptance is the key to serenity. After hugging me through the tears, Craig would tell me to "cowgirl up" and get after it. So tomorrow, I will get up and do more things, because there are more things to do and more people to see and I've got more love to share. I have learned in this season that I'm perfectly capable of managing many things, but I've also learned the best way to honor my husband is by helping others manage their present reality as well. And giving someone else hope is all the reason I need. 💙

Blessed be the God and Father of our Lord Jesus Christ,
the Father of mercies and God of all comfort,
who comforts us in all our affliction,
so that we may be able to comfort those who are in any affliction,
with the comfort with which we ourselves are comforted by God.
2 CORINTHIANS 1:3-4 (ESV)

A Rescue Mission

June 13, 2020

APPEARANCES CAN BE DECEIVING. THE PHOTO that popped up today in my Facebook memories looks like a man on vacation. Happy. Relaxed. Content.

But we were not on vacation. We were on a rescue mission. The poolside hammock in Campeche, Mexico was a trauma-ward gurney. Craig was sick, and we were desperate to get him well.

In the preceding weeks, we had gone to great lengths to extricate ourselves and our business from a lucrative client relationship.

We'd hired expensive attorneys to ensure that we weren't in breach of contract. We willingly turned over our crew and our operations, desperate to pull Craig out of the field as quickly as possible. The work didn't matter. The money didn't matter. We needed to save him. Craig wanted to live.

He hadn't slept more than three hours a night for months, continually ripped from his slumber by horrifying nightmares or debilitating muscle cramps. He was likely malnourished as a result of a limited diet while working six days a week in the north Texas plains, combined with rewired plumbing from a gastric bypass years prior. Only after his death would I learn about the connection between vitamin deficiency and brain function. Take your B_{12}, my friends.

We fled to our favorite city in Mexico with dreams of buying a house and starting fresh. We imagined a slower pace and a home for ministry and fellowship. But Campeche was hot in June, and we hadn't anticipated the afternoon storms. Our previous visits had been in January and April, when you could spend leisurely days strolling through cobblestone streets in the historic city center. On this trip, we limited our walks to early morning and sought refuge indoors to wait out the stifling humidity and midday rains. The excursion was not without its high points, of course. We ate well and visited with friends and created cherished memories. But the elements seemed to conspire against us, and our efforts at relaxation felt forced. We continued to fight an unseen foe as we returned home to Texas.

Still, we kept fighting. We railed against the darkness side by side. And we experienced noteworthy victories. I learned to be more patient, to demonstrate grace, and to humbly ask forgiveness the many times I failed. Craig's friends rallied around him with encouragement and prayers, often spending hours with him on the phone. Craig even slept through the night once or twice.

We also discovered his physical and mental exhaustion had deep roots. Memories of childhood trauma emerged from the recesses of his mind. The lucrative-yet-taxing client project had filled our coffers but also pried open a Pandora's box of pain that needed to be addressed. Craig's counselor was compassionate, our pastor supportive, his doctor pragmatic. The consensus was for him to start on antidepressants, at least for a short season. I hated the idea but wanted to honor Craig's decision. He hated the idea but was desperate for relief.

Four days after starting the prescription, he was gone.

Craig had been on the same medication before, years earlier. But he was forty pounds heavier then, and his body chemistry was different. He wasn't malnourished, sleep deprived, or starved for serotonin. And, although we were aware of the potential side effects, reading the prescribing information from the FDA months after his passing was a kick in the gut:

> Suicide is a known risk of depression and certain other psychiatric disorders, and these disorders themselves are the strongest predictors of suicide. There has been a long-standing concern, however, that antidepressants may have a role in inducing worsening of depression and the emergence of suicidality in certain patients during the early phases of treatment.

The next page states in bold letters:

> **All patients being treated with antidepressants for any indication should be monitored appropriately and observed closely for clinical worsening, suicidality, and unusual changes in behavior, especially during the initial few months of a course of drug therapy, or at times of dose changes, either increases or decreases.**

Monitoring. Close observance. Nobody had told us, yet I can so easily question whether I did enough. Whether I should have canceled my lunch plans the day he passed. Whether I missed any warning signs.

But it started out a good day. Craig took an hour-long power walk in the morning because he knew exercise could increase serotonin in the brain. (You don't exercise when you're planning to die.) He finished writing an essay about sonship in Christ and emailed it to a new mentor in the faith. He journaled that morning about feeling encouraged by a call with a friend who had a potential job lead. And the day before, Craig had scheduled three more appointments with his counselor.

The man in the hammock wanted to live. He loved life. He loved people. Seeing the photo in my social media feed left me momentarily crippled, sobbing at the kitchen table. But then, I decided to write. Love demands action. People need hope.

Sometimes, the chemotherapy doesn't cure the cancer. Sometimes it does. Everyone struggles with depression at one time or another or knows someone who has battled those demons. The ultimate cure is love. If you are struggling today, know that you are worth fighting for. Know we are in this fight together. Craig was a valiant warrior and mighty man of God. He never gave up the fight, and neither will I. Neither should you. Take to heart today his words of exhortation:

"Rise up. Do not quit before the miracle happens."

I believe that I shall look upon the goodness of the Lord
in the land of the living!
Wait for the Lord;
be strong, and let your heart take courage;
wait for the Lord!
PSALM 27:13-14 (ESV)

Back and Forth

July 7, 2020

YESTERDAY WAS THE TWO-YEAR ANNIVERSARY OF never seeing my husband again. Two years since our last kiss goodbye, which was only supposed to be for a few hours. It was the two-year anniversary of never again watching with awe and wonder as he whipped up an incredible dinner from whatever was in the fridge and the pantry or debating whether to just go out for Korean barbecue. It was the two-year anniversary of never coming upstairs and finding him sound asleep on the couch in the media room and gently removing his glasses so he could continue to nap in peace. Two years since the last time we sat in the living room and had coffee before breakfast and compared notes about what we had read in that day's devotional. Two years since I could ever possibly hear, "I've got a surprise for you..."

I write all this not to evoke pity, but because it does not even begin to scratch the surface of describing what was lost on July 6, 2018. The love of my life. My best friend. My business partner. My mentor in the faith. My archnemesis when we argued and my place of refuge in the storm.

My husband.

Yesterday was hard and beautiful and sad and fun and full of grief and full of healing and, ultimately, really good. Like the year before, I left town and sought comfort in the country, in the company of close friends who stood by me that first horrific week when my brain could not even process the trauma and the shock. The four of us spent the last forty-eight hours telling stories, grilling burgers, playing card games, and taking too many pictures of horses in the pasture. The owner of the property we rented has a heart the size of Texas and surprised us upon arrival with a plate of fresh cinnamon rolls waiting in the kitchen. Craig's favorite.

Throughout the day, other dear friends texted and posted words of condolence and comfort and compassion. Not only did they not forget my husband, but they remembered me. I felt seen. I felt understood. I felt loved.

So, once again, I cannot help but count my blessings. I have witnessed new friendships formed—and I have made new friends myself—which never would have come to pass were it not for the tragedy of Craig's passing. I have gone on great adventures and grown stronger in my faith and learned to appreciate the quiet times and places of rest. God makes streams in the desert.

I am grateful to all my friends for walking this journey with me. I am grateful for the countless ways they have demonstrated God's love. For their patience and grace and empathy and encouragement. Every single person who has reached out by phone or text or commented on my blog or simply clicked "like" on a social media post is further evidence that "every good gift and every perfect gift is from above, and comes down from the Father of lights, with whom there is no variation or shadow of turning."

Two are better than one,
because they have a good return for their labor:
If either of them falls down,
one can help the other up.
But pity anyone who falls
and has no one to help them up.
ECCLESIASTES 4:9-10 (NIV)

But they who wait for the Lord shall
renew their strength
they shall mount up with wings like eagles;

they shall run and not be weary;

they shall walk and not faint.

ISAIAH 40:31 (ESV)

Someday Satisfied

August 13, 2020

CRAIG WAS A FOODIE IN EVERY sense of the word. He loved taking friends to funky eateries off the beaten path and creating memories by breaking bread together. At home, he could make anything out of anything and expressed his love through cooking. If I liked a dish at a restaurant, he would figure out how to replicate it. He transformed leftovers into gourmet meals and made a habit of preparing too much brisket so he could share with neighbors.

I miss seeing him moving around the kitchen like a man on a mission. I miss sitting across the table from him at the local diner on Saturday morning and shopping with him at the Korean grocer. I miss seeing the joy in his face when he prepared a new dish and the simple pleasure of sitting down to dinner with the one I love. I crave that connection.

But I know that one day, that craving will be satisfied. I will see Craig again, and we will enjoy a magnificent feast in God's kingdom. Jesus promised His disciples, "I am the bread of life. He who comes to Me shall never hunger, and he who believes in Me shall never thirst" (John 6:35 NKJV). At the marriage supper of the Lamb, our hearts and bellies will be filled with His perfect love, and we will have everlasting joy.

Until then, I can enjoy the sweetness of God's presence right here and find sustenance in His Word. He invites me to the table daily, revealing His love in countless ways. As I take comfort in the promise of what lies ahead, even now, I can taste and see that the Lord is good. 💙

Blessed are you who are hungry now, for you shall be satisfied.
Blessed are you who weep now, for you shall laugh.
LUKE 6:21 (ESV)

Familiar With Suffering

August 19, 2020

YESTERDAY, AN ACQUAINTANCE FROM CHURCH REACHED out to me for guidance. She had met a woman whose son had taken his life and was moved with compassion toward her. The mother was lost and broken, consumed with grief. My friend had wept and prayed with her that day and messaged me in the evening.

"I didn't know what I could tell her right in the middle of her crisis, but I thought of you, and that you are someone who unfortunately knows this road," she wrote. "Can you help me help her?"

We texted for the next hour, and I shared with her many of the insights I had gleaned since losing Craig two years ago. Her expression of concern for a heartbroken mother was itself an act of love, I said. Empathy is a healing balm to those crippled by grief. People often struggle with the subject of death and never quite know how to comfort someone in their loss. They rely on platitudes that promise a better tomorrow or use humor to try and lighten the heavy atmosphere, and in doing so unwittingly invalidate the other person's pain.

But Jesus was a man familiar with suffering. He expressed His anguish openly, pouring out His heart before the Father. The very Son of God sought mercy in His time of need, knowing the Lord is near to the brokenhearted and saves the crushed in spirit (Psalm 34:18). God hears our cries, and He gives us both comfort and strength in our suffering.

We cannot escape the fires of affliction in this life, but we can trust that God will bring beauty from ashes. No tear is wasted, and so often, He uses our pain to bring healing to others. Like silver being purified in the refiner's fire, we can allow the seasons of suffering to remove the dross from our souls. In the process, we come to reflect the image of the One who makes His face to shine upon us. Through divine alchemy, He transforms our pain into compassion, so we can pay it forward with love. 💙

In the days of his flesh,
Jesus offered up prayers and supplications,
with loud cries and tears,
to him who was able to save him from death,
and he was heard because of his reverence.
HEBREWS 5:7 (ESV)

In The Moment

THE FIRST TIME I VISITED CRAIG in Texas, my return flight to New York City was at 6:00 AM. He was gracious enough to drive me to the airport himself, which meant waking up well before dawn to get me there on time. As we stopped for gas on the way to DFW, he casually suggested I go inside to make us each a cup of coffee while he filled the tank. "But I don't want coffee," I replied, matter-of-factly. Craig bristled. "Maybe since I'm driving you to the airport at 4:30 in the morning, I would like some coffee," he said with a sharp tone.

Oh.

When left to my own devices, I can be remarkably thoughtless and lazy. I will default to the path of least resistance and let the combined forces of gravity and lethargy do their thing. That early morning trip to the airport brought a wake-up call, in more ways than one. It was the first time I really understood that being in a relationship was going to take some effort. The warm and fuzzy feelings of being in love would ebb and flow through the course of our marriage, but the opportunities to show love were ever present. Love is doing something for the other person's benefit, even when you don't feel like it.

Last night, I wept over the missed opportunities to love my husband. I cried for all the dishes I left in the sink and the countless times I pretended not to hear the car pull in, so I didn't have to help unload groceries. I cried for the dinners I didn't cook and the activities I rolled my eyes at when Craig just wanted a companion. I know I loved him well, but I could have loved him better.

Love is in the little things. We may not always get a "thank you," but we can always make a difference. We are called to bear fruit, and that means sowing seed in our actions as well as our words. Make the effort. Muster the strength. Because your small act of love today is bigger than you know. 💙

"This is my commandment,
that you love one another as I have loved you."
JOHN 15:12 (ESV

Every Good Gift

January 12, 2021

CRAIG WAS A DREAMER. HE WAS a visionary and consummate entrepreneur. He was notorious for emerging from a long shower with a genius idea for a new product or service that would be a home run in the marketplace. He wrote songs and created recipes, and he had just taken up bagpipe lessons when he passed.

I marvel at his countless accomplishments, but I also grieve for all the missed opportunities and plans put on hold. The songs he planned to record that now remain unsung. The restaurant he wanted to launch that will never open its doors. I think about the fact that the world has been deprived of the joy that would have come through those efforts. And I am reminded to get busy.

When I am lazy or complacent, I remember not to squander the gifts and talents God has given me. When the media clamor around current events pulls me off task, I think about not leaving things undone. I don't want to leave behind half-written books. I don't want to go to my deathbed having never unwrapped the pressure cooker Craig gave me for our last Christmas together or wishing I had finally launched the online course I've thought about for years. I don't want to fall into the trap of assuming there's still time.

We get busy, and life is full of demands. We have a responsibility to our family and employers and friends and community. But we are made in the image of God with the inspiration and ability to create. Steward your talents. Invest in your vision. Honor the gift of today, and let the world experience the fullness of joy God wants to express through you. 💙

Each of you should use whatever gift you have received to serve others, as faithful stewards of God's grace in its various forms.
1 PETER 4:10 (NIV)

For we are God's handiwork, created in Christ Jesus to do good works, which God prepared in advance for us to do.
EPHESIANS 2:10 (NIV)

Counting The Days

June 17, 2021

WHEN I LOST CRAIG, JESUS COULD not come back fast enough. I was obsessed with the rapture of the church and the return of Christ. I watched countless YouTube teachings and dove into Scripture headfirst, trying to discern the date of our departure. I read Old Testament prophecies and looked at historical events that aligned with the signs of the times that Jesus told His disciples would take place.

In the gospels, Christ describes "labor pains" of blood moons and earthquakes, wars and rumors of wars that will herald His return. The promise was both encouraging and frustrating. I wanted a date. I wanted certainty. I wanted relief—to be snatched out of the deep chasm of sorrow up into the clouds of heaven.

In time, however, I stopped obsessing over the calendar. For one thing, it's quite selfish. I wanted to escape my pain, which is understandable, but I was not thinking of millions of others suffering in their own way. I just wanted my broken heart to be made whole. When the church is gone, however, and Christ comes back, time is up. There will be no more time to share the gospel. No more time to ensure the lost sheep come into the sheepfold. And that reality would be exponentially more tragic than my loss.

Knowing the date of Christ's return also does me no good. It has me looking for the exit door, rather than looking for people who need help. Although we are called to discern the times and keep watch, we're not meant to fixate on the future. When I obsess over the date we will be caught up in the clouds to meet the Lord in the air (1 Thessalonians 4:17), I am not focused on my Father's business. Pride and complacency lurk in the shadows.

Jesus told His disciples, "Look, I tell you, lift up your eyes, and see that the fields are white for harvest" (John 4:35B ESV). Every day here is a blessing, every sunrise an opportunity to shine the light of Christ. He comforted me in my affliction and wants that none should perish. My job is to testify to His grace, mercy, and love, so others will desire to know Him too. As much as I am eager to stand before my Savior, I want to make sure that when He comes, I won't be going home alone.

> *Already the one who reaps is receiving wages*
> *and gathering fruit for eternal life,*
> *so that sower and reaper may rejoice together.*
> JOHN 4:36 (ESV)

Strength in the Storm

July 1, 2021

Over the past three years, countless friends have commented on the strength of my faith. They marvel at my resilience and steadfast trust in God in the wake of Craig's passing. The thing is, faith was the only thing that made sense.

We have a choice. When a crisis happens—when our world comes undone—we can stand on God's promises, or we can choose to despair. And why would I choose that? Why would I choose to shake my fist at the God who custom-made Craig just for me and moved heaven and earth to bring us together? Why would I purpose in my heart to toss in the towel?

I never denied my grief or the pain of loss. That pain still resonates. But I chose not to hang my hat on it; I chose not to let sorrow overshadow the goodness all around me. Widowhood was my reality, but I chose not to make it my identity.

Despair doesn't do anyone any good. While I'm still here, I can do my part to make the world a better place—to love my neighbor as myself. Some days are easy. Some days are a struggle. But people need hope, and "I press on toward the goal for the prize of the upward call of God in Christ Jesus" (Philippians 3:14 ESV).

The enemy comes to steal, kill, and destroy. God is bigger. So, I cry, I pray, and I set my thoughts on things above. Death doesn't get the last word. I choose joy. 💙

Do not sorrow,
for the joy of the Lord is your strength.
NEHEMIAH 8:10B (NKJV)

And after you have suffered a little while,
the *God of all grace*,
who has called you to his eternal glory in Christ,

will himself restore, confirm,
strengthen, and establish you.

1 PETER 5:10 (ESV)

The Light Shines in the Darkness

July 8, 2021

CRAIG AND I MET BY PHONE many months before we met in person. The awesome testimony of God's divine intervention that led to our marriage is a longer story for another time. It's a book unto itself. Those early phone conversations, however, laid the foundation for our shared journey. I came to know Craig's humor, his intellect, his creativity and, most importantly, his character. I told my business partner at the time that Craig was "the most godly man I have ever met."

It was a peculiar thing for me to say, given I hadn't yet met Craig in person, and likewise had not yet met Jesus. But six days into my first trip to Dallas, my future husband led me to the Lord—the only One who loved me even more than he did.

Three years ago today, I posted the news of my husband's death on social media. My announcement and the reactions from several friends came up in my Facebook memories this morning. I was struck by how many people commented that Craig was a godly man. Of all the things they remembered—of all the things they could have highlighted—it was his love of Christ and his love of people that left a lasting impression.

I know from our many years together that Craig's deep faith and passion for helping others were born out of his own trials and trauma. Every hardship he overcame heightened his ability to connect and empathize with others, because he could see their pain beneath the surface. He knew the struggle.

Although he is no longer here, I now know my husband better too. I understand how the fires of affliction can draw us closer to God, as worldly concerns are burned away. The only balm for the heartache is the joy of helping others. As I enter my fourth year flying solo, I pray people still see Craig in me, knowing so many could see Christ in him. 💙

In the same way, let your light shine before others,
so that they may see your good works
and give glory to your Father who is in heaven.
MATTHEW 5:16 (ESV)

Unexpected Blessings

December 11, 2021

IN LATE 2019, I SPENT ELEVEN days in Israel with two dozen strangers who became friends. As we traveled the country to see the sites, we gathered at the end of every day for a time of prayer and reflection. Seated in a large circle, we each would briefly share our one "low" and "high" for the day—the thing that hit us hard, and the thing that lifted our spirits. Sharing those thoughts not only helped foster authentic relationships, but it made us mindful of the many blessings and life-changing moments we experience daily.

Tonight, our tour group had its first reunion. Less than half the members could attend, but a dozen of us still gathered at the home of our trip leader, with two more participants and our former guide joining us virtually via Zoom. Stories and recollections of our time together flowed effortlessly in between updates about work and family and holiday plans.

During the evening, we revived the tradition of sharing our highs and lows, but with a twist. We each shared the painful parts of the past two years, but also joyful experiences and unexpected blessings. Hearing each person speak of death and loss was sobering, but the back-to-back testimonies of God's overwhelming goodness were a balm to the soul.

As my turn came around, I summarized the heartache of losing three pets, and the fear that accompanied peculiar health issues. Then I shared about the many moments of deep connection I encountered during and after the shutdowns. I talked about people who went far out of their way to help me through trials. I recounted holiday meals with friends who have become family, weekly walks with a God-gifted sister, and the wisdom gained from my Bible study group.

The more I talked, the more I realized just how remarkable the past two years have been. Jesus told us plainly that we would have tribulation, but He also assured us that He already has claimed the victory. Even as we walk through the valley of the shadow of death, Christ guides us, comforts us, and nourishes our soul. As we closed out our evening with hymns and songs, I could see Scripture come to life. "The light shines in the darkness, and the darkness has not overcome it." 💙

In everything give thanks;
for this is the will of God in Christ Jesus for you.
1 THESSALONIANS 5:18 (NKJV)

I long to see you so that I may impart to you some
spiritual gift to make you strong—that is, that you and I
may be mutually encouraged by each other's faith.
ROMANS 1:11-12 (NIV)

Seasons of Growth

EVERYTHING LOOKS DEAD IN WINTER. THE trees are bare, the grass withered and brown. Time ticks by slowly, as cold winds blow and the landscape is desolate for a season. Then suddenly, often unexpectedly, you catch a glimpse of new life. A crocus peeking its head out of the earth. A red-breasted robin that has made its return. Buds on branches and green leaves unfurling.

This will be my fourth spring without Craig. The year he passed, I was bursting with ideas and overflowing with creative momentum. I could not wait to plant a garden and pursue a bevy of projects that had blossomed in my heart. But I put them on hold because my husband needed me. He needed rest. He needed rescue. He needed my full attention as we battled against unseen forces of darkness.

Then, in the middle of summer, winter came.

He died, and everything around me looked dead too. Hopes and dreams were dry and withered, my spirit parched. Even so, seeds had been planted. They laid dormant for a season, but in time, new life sprang forth. New friendships, new travels, new creative projects, and business opportunities.

We were made to grow. Continual change is part of God's divine plan. Circumstances do not stop Him from moving. Few things flourish in dry ground, so He rains down living waters of mercy and grace. He replenishes our soul in the dark days of winter. The promise of a new season is just around the corner, and when we least expect it, we discover a heart in bloom. 💙

The flowers appear on the earth;
The time of singing has come,
And the voice of the turtledove
Is heard in our land.
SONG OF SOLOMON 2:12 (NKJV)

New Adventures

May 6, 2022

FOR MORE THAN THREE YEARS, I looked at Craig's clothes hanging in our bedroom closet and thought, "I can't." Everything was in the same place as on July 6, 2018, when I left the house to meet a friend for lunch and arrived home to widowhood. For more than three years, his dress shirts, ties, jackets, slacks, and jeans still filled the rung along the left wall. The T-shirts and gym shorts I had most recently washed remained neatly stacked on top of the dresser. Some days, I would grab an armful of my favorite flannel shirts, hug them tight, and lean my cheek against the fabric, wishing that the sharp angle of the hangers underneath was the firm curve of his shoulder. But most days, I just left everything alone, so part of my brain could pretend life was normal. His clothes were in the closet. He'd be home soon.

About a month ago, something shifted. I walked into the closet and thought, "It's time." More than feeling courageous enough to tackle a hard task, I actually felt joyful. I got excited at the idea of donating several items to a ministry that serves men recently released from prison. And I knew that many of Craig's funky bowling shirts would make some local hipsters very happy. I began pulling handfuls of clothing off the rod, sorting garments into piles to be picked up or delivered to new caretakers.

I've been plowing through his wardrobe for a few weeks since, and I have found that letting go gets a little easier with each packed box or bin. But a couple days ago, a thought came to mind that ripped the scab off my grief. My relationship status on Facebook still says "married." That needed to change.

When Craig passed, I left my status untouched both to honor my husband and because it still felt so very real. We were in covenant. The two become one flesh. No matter how much I want to hold fast to the life we shared for more than fourteen years, the moniker is no longer accurate. I am a widow. And I am called to speak truth.

I wanted to kick the can down the road. I even set a calendar item to change my cover photo and relationship status later this weekend. But it's time. Today marks forty-six months since Craig crossed over into heaven, and it's a good milestone. I am, in fact, honoring him by moving forward. By not letting another month go by wearing an identity that no longer fits.

One of the things I love most about Craig is that he was a true Renaissance man. He was a lightning-fast learner and always up for new adventures, from sumo wrestling to singing for the queen. He bounced happily from launching an online television network to inventing cotton candy flavors, and from developing mobile apps to flying drones. If there's one thing Craig would encourage me to do, it would be to make space for something new.

Of course, changing a label on social media has no impact on my limitless love for my late husband. I have grown into the faith-filled, empathetic, and confident person I am today because of Craig's example and his continual encouragement and support. I can see how I have adopted many of his best character traits, as well—the two are still one flesh. So, instead of clinging to the past, I can honor my husband by running headlong into the next season with the boundless enthusiasm I frequently saw in him. And, although changing my status on social media feels like a very bold statement, I know Craig is excited to see what new adventures we'll take on next. 💙

"And the two shall become one flesh."
So they are no longer two but one flesh.

MARK 10:8 (ESV)

Four Years

July 6, 2022

HERE WE ARE. FOUR YEARS. FOUR unfathomable years.

Four years since I came home to the news that crushed my heart to rubble. Four years since I went from wife to widow in an instant. Four years of looking through the same several dozen photos of Craig, frustrated beyond all measure that I'll never be able to take a new picture or make another memory.

I am deeply sad. I am deeply grateful.

Grateful for four years of experiencing God's immeasurable love and grace. Grateful for four years of friends old and new rallying by my side. Grateful for four years of travel and adventures and opportunities I may never have experienced in another context. Of course, Craig and I would have had travel and adventures and opportunities of our own. They would have been utterly amazing and brought me deep joy. But I cannot forsake the goodness of what I have encountered along this detour.

This is not my preferred route. I'd rather be riding by my husband's side. Even going solo, however, I have enjoyed beautiful scenery. I have enjoyed the companionship of Christ, who never left and never will. Even on nights when the tears flowed in tandem with guttural sobs, I could say without hesitation, God is good.

So, here we are. Four years. I miss Craig every day. And every day I give thanks for the privilege of being his bride. I give thanks for the blessing of carrying on our shared calling to help people move from hurt to hope. I give thanks for the sweet reassurance that we will see each other again in a new and different way.

Until then, I will embrace this new and different day. I will enjoy quiet conversations with God and laughter with friends. I will savor good food and beautiful surroundings. Even as I grieve, I will look to July 6th with optimism, in honor of the man who modeled what it means to live life to the fullest.

I love you, Craig Thompson. 💙

The steadfast love of the Lord never ceases;
his mercies never come to an end;
they are new every morning;
great is your faithfulness.
LAMENTATIONS 3:22-23 (ESV)

A Line in The Sand

September 15, 2022

"The thief comes only to steal and kill and destroy. I came that they may have life and have it abundantly"

JOHN 10:10 (ESV)

I HAD TWO SIGNIFICANT CONVERSATIONS THE night of July 6, 2018, a few hours after Craig passed. One was with God. The other was with Satan.

I initiated the latter after the last visitor had left the house and two close friends who were staying over had gone to bed. I was alone in the master bedroom, exhausted by a day spent alternately sobbing and graciously thanking people who had come to offer comfort. But I was not too tired to fight.

Standing in the center of the room, I addressed Satan directly. I didn't see him, but I'm sure he was there. Snickering. Gloating. My voice was firm, as I said defiantly, "You can kill my husband, but you cannot steal my joy."

I made a choice in that moment. I chose to live. Two years would pass before I felt like I had my wits about me again, and another two before I started thinking about what the future might hold. But God declares the end from the beginning, and so did I. This crushing circumstance—this sniper attack from the enemy—would not shake my faith. On the contrary, Satan's scheme to bring me to my knees put me in position to pray. When he tried to knock the wind out of me, my breath carried songs of worship.

I was standing on God's promises. I was clinging to the truth of His Word.

And we know that in all things God works
for the good of those who love him,
who have been called according to his purpose.

ROMANS 8:28 (NIV)

God is not a man, that He should lie, or a son of man, that He should change His mind (Numbers 23:19). He said would bring beauty from ashes, the oil of joy for mourning, the garment of praise for the spirit of heaviness. He promised, and He who promised is faithful.

Am I always happy? No. Have I fought bouts of depression? Absolutely. But I always have joy because I know the battle has been won. Satan was defeated at the cross. Jesus has the keys of death and the grave, and He is seated at the right hand of the Father. Soon and very soon, He is coming back to judge the world with righteousness. I can stand firm in faith because I know my Lord and King.

When your world is falling apart, lean on Jesus. He will be your strength, as you crush the enemy beneath your feet. 💙

And they overcame him by the blood of the Lamb
and by the word of their testimony

REVELATION 12:11A (NKJV)

Looking Up

December 6, 2022

SOME DAYS, I WONDER WHAT CRAIG is doing. Is he keeping busy in heaven, coming up with business ideas for our world that the Lord will share with someone else? Does he have a celestial kitchen to whip up creative cuisine the way he did here on earth? Can Craig come and go along Jacob's ladder, ministering to the broken on another continent, like a Green Beret for God's kingdom?

Does he see me?

In marriage, the two become one flesh. Craig put off his earthly body, but my flesh is still here, and in a way, he still is here, too. I am sure he's busy about the Father's work in some form or fashion I can't understand. But through the deep imprint on my soul, Craig is also busy through me.

Our shared experience in business informs my pursuit of new ventures to bring hope to the hurting through books and speaking. His playful approach to cooking gives me courage in the kitchen and inspires me to share goodies with family and friends. And when I minister to someone experiencing hardship, I hear his words of wisdom leave my lips. The person I am today reflects the person Craig was to me. He taught me to share love more freely.

These are the things I ponder, as the holidays draw near and Craig's birthday approaches. The thought of carrying his legacy gives me comfort. I'm no longer running by his side, but I carry the baton for this last leg of the race. Team Thompson for Team Jesus.

I don't know whether he sees me, but I see Craig in me. The love of Christ connects us still. So, I give him a hug in my heart, as we pass another milestone. His words of encouragement echo in my soul, and I look forward to another day to be about our Father's work. 💙

May he strengthen your hearts so that you will be blameless
and holy in the presence of our God and Father
when our Lord Jesus comes with all his holy ones.

1 THESSALONIANS 3:13 (NIV)

Afterword

IT'S ALL A BLUR. THE BARRAGE of people, food and flowers that filled the house. The decisions made in a mental fog and myriad documents to sign. The packed memorial service and haunting silence in the house the next day. The events in the hours, days, and weeks following my husband's death have begun to fade like an old photograph. Four years is not very long, but from a widow's perspective, it's a broad chasm. It's a lifetime between what was happy and familiar and the new chapter. Not normal, but different. Four years is the vast expanse between the life we were building together and the one just starting to sprout. What will grow depends very much on how we tend the fragile future in the soil of our heart.

A certain variety of Chinese bamboo tree can grow to fifty feet tall. The thick stalks with belly-like nodes along the stem are not only beautiful but can be used as building material. What is unique about this variety, however, is its peculiar growth pattern. Although the seeds will sprout after a few months, it takes about three years for the bamboo to be firmly rooted in the soil. Once it's deeply rooted, the bamboo will begin to put off shoots in the spring and the plant can quickly multiply. But none of that begins to happen until the fourth year.

Four years have passed since my husband ran into the arms of Jesus. Four years filled with friends old and new, vacations and mission trips, conferences, pet projects, and entrepreneurial endeavors. Most importantly, four years of growing in faith by reading God's Word, listening for His voice, and learning how to pray.

After four years of sowing in tears, I am ready to reap in joy. The desire to once more embrace life's possibilities feels unfamiliar; the thought of loving again downright risky. Yet, life is meant to be a grand adventure. God brought Craig into my life through the most peculiar circumstances. He has introduced me to remarkable friends and colleagues through divine appointments and fueled my soul with trips across the globe.

We are meant for connection. We are meant to use all our senses. Jesus came to give us life and life abundantly. To the full and overflowing. When you have lost someone you love, you never move on, but you can choose to move forward. You can choose to embrace God's purposes in their wholeness, knowing He is unfailingly good.

That is my choice, and I pray it's yours too. As I look to the far horizon with a hopeful heart, the love of Christ compels me to move forward. His mercies are new every morning. So, today and every day, I choose life. 💙

She who is truly a widow, left all alone,
has set her hope on God and continues
in supplications and prayers night and day.
1 TIMOTHY 5:5 (ESV)

Resources

SUICIDE PREVENTION

If you or someone you know is struggling with depression or suicidal thoughts, help is available. The 988 Suicide & Crisis Lifeline provides free and confidential emotional support to people in suicidal crisis or emotional distress 24 hours a day, 7 days a week, across the U.S.

Simply call or text 988 to connect with trained counselors who can listen, offer support, and provide access to additional resources if necessary. To learn more, visit **www.988lifeline.org**.

GRIEF COUNSELING

GriefShare support groups meet weekly to provide compassionate support for anyone grieving the death of a family member or friend. Thousands of groups currently operate in cities and towns across the U.S. and Canada, and you can join any time. To find a GriefShare group in your area, visit **www.griefshare.org**.

You can also find additional resources on the GriefShare website, including books and personal study materials, and sign up for daily emails, which offer hope and practical information to help with the recovery process.

Hope for Widows Foundation provides private online support, resources, and caring advocacy for women nationwide who are learning to move forward after losing their spouse. The organization builds community through online and in-person meetings and its award-winning Hope for Widows Blog and offers grant funding to help offset the financial challenges many widows experience.

Visit **www.hopeforwidows.org** to get involved, apply for a grant, read inspiring blog essays, and find out about events and special programs the organization has available.

www.ingramcontent.com/pod-product-compliance
Lightning Source LLC
Chambersburg PA
CBHW070722130626
46553CB00005B/2106